The Extinction of the Marriage Covenant : Fact or Fiction

By Shelia T. Cisco

WestBow Press books may be ordered through booksellers or by contacting:

WestBow Press
A Division of Thomas Nelson & Zondervan
1663 Liberty Drive
Bloomington, IN 47403
www.westbowpress.com
844-714-3454

All Scripture quotations are taken from the NEW AMERICAN STANDARD BIBLE®, Copyright © 1960, 1962, 1963, 1968, 1971, 1972, 1973, 1975, 1977, 1995 by The Lockman Foundation. Used by permission.

ISBN: 979-8-3850-2884-9 (sc)
ISBN: 979-8-3850-2885-6 (e)

Library of Congress Control Number: 2024913518

Print information available on the last page.

WestBow Press rev. date: 08/27/2024

WESTBOW
PRESS®
A DIVISION OF THOMAS NELSON
& ZONDERVAN

The Extinction of the Marriage Covenant : Fact or Fiction

This year I was told by a young woman who was born in 1995, that marriage is a dying institution. That is the traditional marriage between a man and a woman. Couples who embark on the traditional marriage route are faced with a barrage of situations that may cause them to reflect on the feasibility and profitability of marriage. Mind you I have said nothing of love. It amazes me that when I interview senior Americans who are in their eighth or ninth decade of life. I found that some of these individuals were married on the average of 65-72 years. I also found that even those who had remarried because of death of a spouse were content in their second **marriage and had marital longevity. This book is dedicated to those who are** contemplating marriage. Whether this is your first marriage or not I want you to ask yourself this question. Am I embarking on a contract or a covenant?

Dedication

This book is designed to encourage the next generation on the marriage covenant. A plethora of Godly examples will be depicted in longevity and purpose. Most marriages span multiple decades some have been married for fifty plus years. What is their secret? Most of the couples interviewed in this book proudly proclaimed that they put God first in their marriages. A few to my surprise were not always equally yoked. But due to the wife's obedience most husbands came to know the Lord before their deaths. We will be presented with women who were married, widowed and those we have been divorced. Those who remarried were blessed with longevity in their marriages and favor of God showered down upon their lives. Contract or covenant, which will it be for you and your family's legacy.

My most precious example of marriage came from my parents Johnnie and Ethel Mae Wilson. My mother was married twice. She was married to each husband until their deaths. They both treated my mother like a queen. My aunt Mildred Ramsey was married 50 years to her husband Curtis Ramsey. Her eldest daughter Barbara Ivy has been married to her husband Jake for 58 years. I have a dear cousin who was married in her youth and is still married to this day Evelyn Joyce Burk- Jones has been married to the love of her life Reginald Jones for 53 years.

My cousin Brenda Taylor and her husband David have been married for 45 years. I once thought that longevity is marriage does not occur in African – American families. That is a false belief created by the media. In Afro-centric households, the culture often falls prey to the depiction of death, divorce and men leaving their families. That is why the urgency to celebrate marriages is paramount in the Afro-centric community. The legacy of the single parent household has been propagated since the days of slavery and it is time we change this narrative.

Now you cannot be married for any length of time without going through some trials and tribulations. Sickness and health that is what the traditional vows said. Cupboards full and some empty refrigerators. Our parents came through it with prayer and fasting. Younger couples may feel the need to omit their traditional vows and write their own. I appreciate the sentiments. But it is through the test of our faith, that marriages come through fireproof. Many survived health diagnosis that would have shaken most people. I have seen women walk away from husbands who were diagnosed with cancer but not these people of God. I have knowledge overflowing from watching the lives of theses woman. I thank God for these Godly examples. I author this book today to encourage our young people. Marriage is not an outdated institution. God ordains it. He set marriage up as a covenant relationship and not a contract. Marriage like any other fundamental relationship can be maligned with distractions. Individuals who are married are often compared to single individuals which is a mistake. Single women and married women have little in common. Except that they are women. A person who has decided to stay single are living under a distinct set or codes and ethics than married women. The following paragraphs will explore this in detail. Prepare for The Extinction of Marriage Covenant: Fact or Fiction

Engagement may be presented in two ways. A contract (business transaction or a covenant).

vii

If you are a person with substantial wealth and securities, this proposed engagement may be presented as a contract. If both parties have substantial wealth within themselves, they may be looking at a marriage contract. Now if both parties are starting off on the same financial footing so to speak then a covenant agreement should be considered. If both parties are individuals of faith and believe marriage is not a contract but a sacred service ordained by God, then they will govern themselves accordingly. Now let us take another look at those couples who were married sixty plus years. It is obvious that these marriages took place before prenuptial agreements were a concern to protect marital assets. It is also plausible that the man was the main provider of the household. Many cases couples married the 1940's, it was understood that the woman would run the household and the man would be the provider of the family. My parents were married in 1956. My mother worked only to aid my father. He was the primary breadwinner. When my parents started a business together my mother worked beside my father. They worked together until his health declined. Looking back at their marriage I am certain it was never easy related to the era in which they raised their family. That being the years following the Civil Rights Movement. You see they both were born in the south. They migrated to the north to start a new and better life for their family being people of color. It is my premise that had their marriage been based on a contract and not covenant that they could not have survived the situations that later occurred in their lives. Faith based couples who are contemplating marriage, should search the Word of God for guidance on marital relationships. All that glitters is not gold. Yet relationships that are forged in the furnace of adversity and trials: will come out as pure gold. If one embarks on the road to marital bliss be not naive. You will have trials. Test trials are not designed to destroy a marriage but make it stronger.

Honeymoon

Paradise, the island warm temperate weather, white sands, blue skies, and gentle tropical breezes that caress your body with warm midst form the ocean, room service with the ever present do not disturb sign. Long walks on the beach, delectable dishes, and housekeeper service. A beautiful moon light sky with ten billion stars shing just for you and the love of your life. (Of –course everyone else can enjoy the sky as well). We wish we could live there forever. The honeymoon or yearly vacations allow us to connect with our spouse in an intimate way. I am not just taking about intercourse. Intimacy in the purest sense of the word is a connection of body mind and spirit. One flesh.

Many people confused sexual activity with intimacy. I would like to clarify this point for those who do not know the difference. A man is lonely in a city he just moved to for his job. He decides to take a drive now what he has been told is the Red-Light district. He is looking for a lady of the evening to spend the night with him. (This illustration is for clarity, not for religious debate). He finds a young willing woman. Offers her a price which she accepts or declines. They go to her hotel of choice where she feels that she will be safe. They engaged in sexual intercourse. He pays her and never sees her again. That was sexual intercourse is the rawest form. The man had no prior connection with the woman. He had a sexual desire and lust for a woman he did not know. He committed a sexual act. This is not true intimacy, one may equate it to animalistic behavior, unfortunately these kinds of careless acts can cause the demise of a marriage. Not to mention the sexual diseases that he may bring home to his wife.

When a couple starts to date, they discover they have shared interest. Individuals often meet at work sites, church, or other civic organizations. They find they like the same things; they might have even visited some of the same places. They might take joy and sharing new experiences together. When my husband and I first started dating we shared some first. Let me preface this by saying my husband was a workaholic. He had no outside interest except church. One of our first was him going to the movies with me. Yes, you heard me right. He had never been to the movies in America.

Another first was me introducing him to bowling. Again, something so common still he had not done so, until he met me. These first created for us levels of intimacy. While dating we often would take drives in the country go to local stores and markets. These also created a level of intimacy, as we would talk and share our hopes and dreams for the future. It is during these times when couples are building memories and creating patterns that intimacy. We are most vulnerable with each other during these times as we share our secrets.

faults and failures. We are completely and utterly placing the substance of who we are with another individual. It is during this time that the male may believe that this woman who he has shared his heart with" is bone of is bone and flesh of his flesh."

Intimacy with your partner, spouse, wife is predicate on your desires and her need to satisfy those desires because they came from you. When a wife has this mandate, she knows instinctively how to satisfy and please her husband. She understands how to create a home that becomes his place of refuge restoration and safety. I find what most husbands do not understand is the woman ability to replicate or reproduce seed. Yes, a woman's can be blessed to produce children, but she is also a vessel that reproduces what is planted in her spirit and psyche. If a husband is blessing his wife, she will in turn bless him and his children. As whatever he plants into the woman will reproduce. If a spouse is encouraging and nurturing that is what he will receive from his wife. A woman will always reproduce what has been planted into to her by her parents and her spouse. She will be a fruitful vine in his life. Not just in producing heirs but resources, commerce, and business. She will become that Proverbs 31 woman.

Proverbs 31: verse 10 NASB An excellent wife who can find her?

For her worth is far above jewels.

Verse 11, The heart of her husband trust in her. This speak volumes about connection and intimacy of marriage. It is here that we see the value of a woman who not only fears God, but also see her ministry of marriage in the full context of what it means to her family and community. No wonder Satan fights against the family and the church of the living God!

If a man only sees his wife as clearly a sexual object he is missing the point. A man who is connected to his spouse, is aware that she brings him honor everywhere she goes. Women who demean themselves to keep up with the culture of this world are missing the point. This also goes for those who call themselves the bride of Christ. Married women who are redeemed by the blood of the Lamb, need not to expose themselves as women who do not serve the Lord.

I am a married woman of a certain age with adult children. I respect my husband, myself, and my children to dress in a manner that is not damaging to our relationships. If you were raised in church, you have a conviction that tells you what is proper to wear if you chose to honor your spouse Your spouse family and yourself.

Wearing Dignity

Dignity is a word that has lost its value in our modern-day society. When I look at examples from African – American Culture, specifically in our heritage. I see that dignity was highly valued during the struggle for people of color to gain recognition. One movie that depicts this is the Malcome X story. The nation of Isam presented themselves as orderly. Clean and discipline men marching through the city. Martin Luther King, WEB Debois, Charles Roberson, Mahala Jackson. Marion Anderson are just some of the examples of dignity. Wearing dignity is a choice and a calling. Especially for women. Is easy to lose one's selves in Babylon. Social media entices us to conform the latest style, fashion and wave that is prevalent in society. If one chooses not to follow the crowd; they are seen as uncoordinated with society.

Here is an example of confusing representation. One day I see this sight and I just must share it, as it shows my point. Imaging that you are driving through town. The town has a large Caucasian population. There is a small population of people of color. You see a large Caucasian man leaving a bar. You noticed he was about to lose his pants. No really, he was sagging just like a hip hop artist on BET.

What was your first thought when I described this man?

He was in the wrong part of town. He was drunk. Did he own a belt a belt? Or was he confused about his representation? None the less when I saw him, I was confused, as I did not understand what he was trying to convey. His lack of dignity caused me to feel uncomfortable and lock the doors and windows as I drove by that street.

Strangely women who stand for God who dress in a manner that does not reflect God give off the same message. If a women's speaker approached the pulpit dressed like R and B hip -hop artist on tour how seriously would you take her message. That is if you stayed to her speak.

Long before I reached this period in my life, young men and women would call me Ma'am. I was taken aback at times until I realized it to be a term of respect. In Africa and other parts of the world, I may be called Auntie or Momma. Again, showing reverence and status. The marriage status should also be shown reverence as God ordains it. This goes back to the first man and woman according to the bible. She was bone of his bone and flesh of his flesh. They were one flesh. The opinion of being one in marriage is contrary to widespread belief. The idea of a couple staying together until death appears out of date by today's standards. Younger couples plunge into matrimony for the time being, understanding that the half of the marriages end in divorce. Modern culture often denounces marriage as an institution. Palimony has replaced marriage without the restrictions of traditional covenant. Open marriages now seem more accepting, as to say that one person cannot fulfill the needs of his or her partner. Does one think that traditional marriage has expired in America? Covenant or Contract. Everything in our culture is a contract. Hiring a plumber, someone to complete your landscaping. We hire contractors to complete houses and churches, what about contracts for marriages?

Do we need contracts for marriages? Many Americans would say yes. Especially if you are a person with resources and wealthy. Does attaching a contract to the marital relationship make it more of a business than a lifetime partnership? Does having this contract replace love and commitment? Does it provided assurance for the children that their parents will be with them through all the developmental stages? The answer to this and many questions hinge on the status of culture faith and the belief that marriage was ordained by God. Many Americans no longer believe in the God of the bible therefore, the belief that marriage is ordained by God viewed as antiquated.

Open Marriages.

I admit that I was raised in a period where there was one couple in the house for a lifetime. My culture also has something to do with this as well as my faith based – community. Marriage was seen as the most esteemed position in society. A man was judged by the fact that he had a family and wife to support. He appeared more stable and serious minded because of the station he held in life. Imagine a woman attending a dinner party held by her corporation and introducing both of her husbands to the boss. I wonder how long she would last in that company. Would her corporate status be taken away because she chose to have an open marriage? Most people will tell you that these are private issues and not up for discussion. It only becomes an issue when custody concerning minor children are involved. Open marriages are not something new. They even existed in biblical times. One of the Greatest kings in Israel lived in open marriages.

I am speaking about none other than King Soloman. One man who was married to seven hundred women and had three hundred concubines. If we say he loved women that would be right. His desires to have every woman he saw had severe consequences for himself and the nation of Israel at that time.

Have we lost the honor in marriage as a society, or do we view it as another milestone in development? Virginity and marriage were seen as the highest dedication to God. Many young women have given away their virginity not fully understanding that it is a gift to be given to their husbands in marriage.

Modern culture demeans a woman who chooses to save herself for her husband. Celibacy by choice is seen as a woman who is frigid or unlovable. The truth however may surprise you. Unfortunately, many women were robbed of this gift due to rape or incest. They could never trust a man again related to the way their virtue was taken from them.

It is no wonder that many view virginity as something of antiquity. There are some mothers who are surprised to know that their daughters were virgins when they were married as they assumed they were not related to today's standards. Culture and societal pressures can have a negative effect on a young woman's self-esteem. Social media enhances showing the worse parts of your life desirable. Society also has depicted various races as loose not having morals. Historically speaking Black women and children were raped upon slave ships before ever reaching the new world. The African – American female was cultural assaulted of her virginity continued long after Jim - Crow was abolished in the south. It is no wonder that the sacredness of a Black woman's virginity, is dismissed as something that society dismissed as non-existent. That in conjunction with fathers missing from the homes either from death or incarceration; have robbed many young girls of the security and protection of a father. Some who chose to walk away from their families continuing the legacy of single mothers brought about during slavery. Yes, slavery was the undoing of the Black family. When mothers and fathers were sold away from their children. The virtue of a Black female child was always at stake.

Many women have been exploited by their own family members and forced into sexual acts and trafficking. It is important for each woman to express their own trauma and seek counseling before going into a marital relationship. It is possible to carry the unwanted stress guilt and regret of such actions in one's marriage. A woman may feel embarrassed by her past molestations and feel uncomfortable sharing that with her future spouse. The closeness and sincerity of their relationship will let her know when she is able to share that information. As women we often walk around with a closet full of secrets fearful of what others may think of us. Women have borne the shame of rape and molestations from the beginning of time. This even occurred in biblical times.

Virtue is from God and man will not be able to take that from you. No matter what men have tried to do to you in your past, God is able to restore your virtue. Just as Jesus forgave an Adulterous woman in John 8:1-11 NASB He can heal and restore you. You may have felt dirty and unclean much like the woman with the issues of blood in Matthew 9:18-22 NASB.

God can heal you and restore you to a spirit of purity. I find that when ministering or praying with young women that many do not realize who are in Christ. They carry to weight of their past even when they were not at fault into their future relationships. Rape incest and molestations are designed to convince you that you are unworthy of the God kind of love. This is far from the truth!

You no longer must carry another person's sin against your body for the rest of your life. You can be restored in the true love of God. Restoration is from the heart of God. Man will attempt to convince you otherwise. That it is something that you must work at, but Christ died for our emotional, physical, and spiritual restoration. It is not up to man but up to you and your trust in the God kind of love that heals and restores pain and can prepare you for a life of marriage.

Protecting your peace something of a new age mind set. A woman who is protecting her peace is really saying I will not let you violate me again. I am strong enough to walk away from those who do not nurture or cherish me as an individual. All throughout history women have been thought of as second-class citizens and Black women even less. I remembered when I first viewed the original "The Color Purple" written by

Alice Walker. My first thought I was glad I was not raised during that time and in the South. My second thought was I would have been killed for retaliating against such a sexist and racist system. There is a scene in the movie where Mister wants to reconcile with Miss Ciley. She tells him "We are better off to be just friends." I thought to myself what a strong woman after all the wrong he did to her. She refused to let him put her in bondage again through emotional sexual and physical abuse. You might be confused about the sexual abuse of their relations, thinking that they were supposed to be married. But Miss Ciley told Sugg Avery that she did not know what it was to be loved, as when Mister was on top of her" I just feel like he is doing his business on top of me." How sad is that!

Miss Ciley was in a marriage that only benefitted Mister and Not Miss Ciley.

Bone of My Bone

You know those couples who are so intrinsically aesthetically interwoven that they feel each other's pain. They are so interwoven that they complete each other's sentences. While the one is thinking I need to order pizza for dinner the other has completed the call, and the order is at the front door. They are connected in a unique way. This occurred months before the wedding vows took place. It might have occurred during the courtship. They began to sense one another's intuitive thought patterns in just a few months because they had a connection. He began working the soil while she was still thinking about what to plant. She began shopping for his antiquated wardrobe. While he planned a momentous vacation that would take her breath away. Neither had attended a class on being one flesh but before they came together as spouses in the legal sense, they became one in the Eyes of God. God prepared the husband for the wife. While she was singled, she prayed for what she wanted in her husband. His character, his traits, and his dedication to God. The man also prayed for what he wanted in a wife. He might have prayed for an excellent cook and a creative stay-at-home parent and a woman with a mind for business. When I ask my husband about his actions. He reminds me you prayed for me before you met me. I am what you prayed for, and he is right!

Let us look at Sara and Dalton

Sara was propitiative to the needs of others by her profession. Like many in her family she served others in the community. Cooking was her forte she provided meals for the community emergencies for the homeless and those who recently lost a loved one.

She found Dalton to be a resource as well as her best friend. She had moved to the mid-west and really had no one to confide except Dalton. The coworkers in their office called him a gentleman. And he was in every sense of the word. He was so gentle that he was often taken advantage by those he cared deeply about. Sara found herself wanting to be with him every day during the courtship. His gentle demeanor refreshed her like a gently breeze coming in off the Atlantic Ocean.

Dalton and Sara were drawn together by as it seemed a divine force, beyond their control. They were so similar yet vastly unique in their individual perspectives. Sara, a culinary delight catered events in her hometown. Dalton was an esteem professor at the community college where he taught for 10 years. The couple could not engage in social circles in places of worship or secular events without his former students approaching him as remarking that he was the best professor they had ever met. This made Sara feel noticeably confident that she was with the right person.

Dalton and Sara were both called to be missionaries. They wanted to return to his homeland and work with individuals estranged from American Charities. Sara had done missionary work in the past in the DRC (Democratic Republic of the Congo). Sara felt when she was there that this was the missing peace in her ancestry. Her siblings feared she might move to Congo, as she felt so welcomed and at peace there. Dalton was also ministry mined sending money back to relatives in Liberia who had no minister of financial security. Dalton figured out when people in his country were poor, they were destitute. They were not waiting on monthly checks from the government or link cards. They were waiting the rainy season to subside so that they could plant their crops. Those who had land. The others depended on the kindness of family members in America and other parts of the world to send financial aid so that they might subsist on merger fare.

Sara and Dalton, both missionaries from diverse cultures would soon learn the heartaches and perils that awaited them following their calling to the mission field.

It was 1989 when the AIDS epidemic arrived at the eastern coast of Africa. Young girls who were often raped by AIDS infected men began producing children who were born with the HIV virus. This massive health crisis affected the already devasted economy.

Sara and Dalton desired to have children. Sara was unable to conceived as a result from her previous lifestyle. They prayed that God would bless them with children. A baby girl was found born with the HIV virus. They knew that this was the answer to their pray. Sara and Dalton knew this child would bring joy to their lives but also reminded Sara of her careless lifestyle as a youth. It was only the mercy of God that kept her from contracting the HIV or AIDS virus. They worked together raising money to come back to America.

Dalton would be found baking and selling bread before classes in the morning. He would also cut lawns with a manchette for some of the academic professions of the college. He was so excited to be attended the university with hopes of coming to America to complete his theology degree. Yes, Dalton and Sara were as different as night and day, but one thing they had in common was their love for God and his church and each other. As strenuous as his studies were he never stopped loving his wife. And she continued selling his baked goods to support the family. Soon they were blessed to have children of their own. The consequences of her youth did not stop her conception or her ability to delivery health off -spring. She was grateful that she had been spared the dreadful infertility that the doctors had pronounced upon her. God had healed and restored her body. It was a new life for her and her husband. The sins of the past had indeed been washed away. New life flowed through their marriage like a waterfall in the tropics. They had found God and each other and were thankful every day to wake-up every day more in love than when they first met. Sara and Dalton raised their family and worked in the ministry together for 40 years. When they retired, they noticed a shift in the relationship. Things that once became a source of laughter began to agitate Sara. She began to pull away from her husband an get involved in other groups that took her focus away from her husband. Although some should call them season saints they were not shielded from the attacks on the enemy. They did not realize it at the time, but they were losing ground. Spiritually and with each other. Dalton began to feel resentful of Sara's self-help groups and her women's prayer circle. He would say" Why don't you all pray at the end of the day instead of first thing in the morning? This prayer thing is interfering with our intimate time together." Sara rebuked her husband and told him that the pray group need to pray in the mornings. This was especially true on Sundays before worship. Dalton reluctantly agreed. Souls were needed in the kingdom. He would have to wait to be intimate with his wife until after church. Sara felt that she needed to abstain from sexual relationship with her husband so that she gives her best to God and be open to minister to his people. The war between the flesh and the spirit seem to always manifest itself before service on Sundays. Why could not Dalton understand that on the days Sara was to minister she gave herself over to God and abstained from fleshly desires. So that God may use her to reach his people. She loved her husband but loved God more. This reminded Sara of her late husband who always chastised her for her commitment to the church and her calling.

It was a tug of war everyday with her late husband. Edgar had been deceased for almost 20 years, but his voice still echoed in her subconscious." You are following this White man's religion and think you are going to heaven because you give your money to the church." Edgar was misguided in his religious upbringing. He was a son of a Baptist preacher who gave into the temptations of the flesh. Edgar's father drank after Sunday services. Sara prayed that the demon of Alcoholism would not grab a hold of his children. Substance abuse and chronic health conditions currently ran her late husband's family. Sara's battle with Edgar ended with his premature death from his addictive lifestyle. Edgar left Sara with two children whom she prayed for daily would not gravitate to the generation's sins of her late husband and his lineage. The sins had also wreaked havoc on each of Edgar's siblings' lives. Sickness and disease followed their addictions from Coronary Artery Disease, Hypertension, Diabetes, and liver failure. Yet, they enjoy the pleasures of sin but if only for a season. Sara tried to model health and wellness practices for her children despite their lineage.

Yes, the war between the flesh and the spirit always seemed to surface just before a breakthrough for Sara. She realized a month after she married Edgar that they were not on the same page. They were complete opposites.

But Sara tried to make the marriage work despite his clear addictions. She divorced Edgar and remarried him a year later. She felt strongly about divorced being a woman of Faith and prayed for Edgar's deliverance. Unfortunately, Edgar had chosen his addictions over his family and sealed his fate. Now Sara, only thought of him when the clear war of the flesh became a struggle again in her home. When Sara reflected on her life with Edgar, she realized that they never had premarital counseling. Sara thought because they were both raised in the church that was enough for them as a foundation. She realized latter that she was wrong.

Dalton was unlike Edgar, yet when he wanted his wife, church, bible study or prayer had to be put on hold. Sara, soon realized why the Apostle Paul, said that he wished all adults were as he was single. Giving himself to God. It was ironic when single women wanted to be married, they rushed into marriage not valuing their singleness. Most did not realize that singleness was a gift to be enjoyed. That way one could give themselves wholeheartedly to God. Strangely in Sara's denomination, singleness as a gift was never taught. Sara noted that most young women after high school were married. Few went to college, and some went to trade school. A few other single women were career oriented. Still, Sara noted that two women in her church did not show the slightest inclination towards matrimony. They were blazing a new trail as professionals. They were very independent and provided for themselves very well. Sara wanted to be like them as they seem to function above societal rules of singleness. Sara noted that singleness was not a curse but a blessing.

It would not be long before Sara's prayers would be answered as Dalton died suddenly in a car accident. Sara, thought to herself, that is not want she wanted. She just wanted to tell Dalton to goodbye, or how meaningful their lives had been. She was widowed for a second time. It took her six months to navigate her new status. She tried to reminisce on the last time she was widowed, but this was different. She was no longer a young woman; she was seasoned with solitude and reflection. She wept bitter tears for her regrets.

Another look at Singleness

Sarah was newly divorced woman in her mid-thirties. She had lived her life for the church. She often felt it would be better if her ex-husband were deceased, still she wished him no harm. She prayed for reconciliation even though her ex-husband betrayed their marital covenant. She felt her church community as well as her inner circle had let her down. Sarah came unstable in mind as well as spirit. Decision making became extremely difficult and she swayed between reality and her desires for reunification of her family. Her associations started to pull away from her sensing that she was headed towards a mental breakdown, and not knowing what to do help her. No one knew what caused the marital discord not even her closest friends. Yet, Sarah thanks to the no fault divorced rules found herself homeless and without means for the first time in her life. Those who tried to aid her in her new life often felt ill equipped to oversee a newly divorced woman. Sarah's emotions were so raw and all over the place at the same time. Her pray group was the first to notice her rocky state of mind. One by one they disappeared. Sarah thought it was because they lacked spiritual insight. But in fact, they could see that she was dealing with something that neither one of them wanted to address. The inner circle wanted to protect their own marriages. It appeared if one person were on the verge of divorce the others would follow suit. It was like and ever-growing plague or cynicism and discontentment, which disrupted marriages. So, one by one they left the inner circle and Sarah was alone for the first time in her life.

Solace with life changes take time to understand. One's identity can change with the stroke of a pen. She was once a wife, now everywhere she looks is filed with strive. The isolation of desolation starts to take its toll on the psyche. When Sarah looked in the mirror, she did not know who it was looking back at her. Sarah's identity was always connected with her husband since she was 19 years old. Now she must reinvent herself. The once married woman noticed that during this whole unpleasant experience that she had gained weight. A friend of her told her that stress and poor sleeping habits were to blame. Which is why she did not recognize herself when she looked in the mirror. Who was this woman that no one wanted, least of all her ex-husband? She tried not to be bitter and continued to protect his reputation. She even moved to another city. No one would know her there. She would just blend in with the rest the middle-aged women. Strangely enough she did not feel middle age. Of -course if this was the 1400's, she might even be considering an old woman. Her spirit had aged despite her youth. This process even though no fault of her known carried its weight on her countenance. What would she tell people when they asked about her family? Would she claim to be divorced or widowed. It all felt the same. She battled with depression. She started hiding away from people. She was careful not to get too close to a different sex. As she was still a woman scorned. She smelled like smoke in her mind as she was smoldering under the injustice that was projected on her newly found status. The Rejected woman never thought at this time in her life she would be alone. She found herself hiding in a mountain retreat away from prying eyes and wagging tongues. She hid this way for several months until the anger pasted and was replaced with brokenness. She had no desire to eat or sleep. She began hearing voices in the night telling her to kill herself as she had nothing to live for, not even her older children wanted to be bothered with her. She regurgitated the situation like a cow chewing it cud. If she could afford to take a shuttle to the moon she would, but she had not thought about getting into the lottery until it was too late. Sarah knew she needed help but was afraid to ask. Each passing day she plunged deeper into despair. She went through the emotions to get her food and managed to pay rent from what she had left after the divorce. But that would not last long and she needed to pull herself together to get a job and make a living. Just maybe a new job is what she needed to move past this divorce thing. Sarah asked around and found out there was a reception job opening next week. This was the break she had been waiting for, she just had to convince herself that she could do this. She needed to put the past behind her and start fresh with a clean slate.

The Single Man

Robert was a forty something man with a fantastic job and a live-in girlfriend. He felt that marriage was a trap and kept his relationship with his live in at arm's length. They rarely shared anything together. It was just a matter of creature comforts. She would go with him to his office party, and he would do likewise. They have had this arrangement for the past five years. Marriage was never mentioned by either of them. They did not want children and really, they were just tolerating each other after five years. His live in Jamie, started to stay out late and not come home after work. Robert could see the signs but told himself she was experimenting with someone else. Two weeks later she moved out without an explanation. Robert spent the whole weekend binged drinking and passed out of the couch. His dog woke him up the next morning barking. Robert let the dog out in his fenced in yard. Then he relieved himself and took care of is morning hygiene. He looked around the vacant apartment and started to realize what had just happened. He saw this coming and did nothing about it. He cared about Jamie, but he never really loved her, and she must have gotten tired of waiting. He could not blame her she wanted better for herself. Robert could hear the dog barking, so he let him in and went to the refrigerator to get his farmhouse blend dog food. It was just the two of them now, as he ascertained his situation of life without commitment.

He would get over Jamie, mentally he was already over her. He was just alone and did not know what to do about that. The outdated institution of marriage that he considered it, never crossed his mind. His parents were divorced when he was five years old. He remembers spending alternate weekends at each of his parent's homes and never wanted that for his children. So, avoiding marriage was the best way, to control that situation. Robert felt justified in his perceptions as most of his friends' parents were also divorced and some of them on their second or third marriage after divorce. Yes, for Robert marriage was just a contract. The sooner he faced that the better! Even so he would never allow himself to get that close to anyone. The closest he came to showing Jamie any affection was giving her a watch for Christmas after being together for two years. He would recover from this and move onto his next live-in girlfriend. Who she was it did not matter? It was a matter of creature comforts.

The Vows

1Corinthians 13: 4-7 NASB "Love is patient, love is kind and, it is not jealous: it does not brag, it is not arrogant. It does not act disgracefully, it does not seek its own benefit; it is not provoked, does not keep an account of a wrong suffered It does not rejoice in unrighteousness, but rejoices with the truth. Love does not delight in evil but rejoices with the truth. It always protects, always trust, always hopes, always preservers.

Some may say that is a tall order and theses are antiquated thoughts on marriage. It is no wonder the divorce rate is at 50 percent in the church as well as in society. No fault divorces are on the rise, one no longer needs a reason to divorce their spouse. An attorney may hear from a spouse that the woman he married no longer can meet my needs. We have just grown apart. A woman can divorce her husband if he is impotent in some states. Although this condition can often be improved with medication and counseling. Our society is a culture of instant -self-gratification will not wait.

Many couples who were once in love so much that they could not keep their hand off each other have replaced their love of each other with objects. Sex-toys have replaced the spouse in many relationships. A husband may start an on-line relationship to meet his sexual desires. He may also suggest and open relationship bringing multiple couples into their marital space. Pornography has taken up residence in many homes as the accepted way of getting ones needs met. I find it interesting that couples in these situations have forgotten what drew them together in the first place. I belief that it was more than outward appearance. Whether in a church community or not couples should seek marital counseling before getting married. Many couples missed this first step, so when the ocean gets rocky, they look to jump overboard. Mature couples who have weathered the storms of life will tell couples that the honeymoon stages do not last forever. Life happens to us all, but how we manage it another story.

Date night is a crucial factor in keeping the relationship growing and vibrant. Scrolling on social media, my heart always leaps for joy when I view couples with longevity. This is an accomplishment that many people overlook. I have many cousins who are in faith -based communities who have been marriage 50-70's years and more. You may say that was in another time and place. Yes, it is true they were married in the 1960's. But that does not mean they were not faced with the same temptation and struggles that other couples face. Things like pornography looked different then, but it was still around. A man who had a mistress then is no different from one having one now, except it is more expensive. Lest you think I am biased in this I am not; I understand that women also get restless in their marriages as well. Whether it is because of lack of affection, being bored with their spouse or medical issues that they are unable to manage. As I said life happens to us all. That is why there are professionals that individuals can go to when they are struggling medical and intimacy issues in their marriages. People of faith may find it difficult to speak to someone about their intimacy issues, especially if they are in leadership in the church.

Servant-Leaders

Let me tell you something Pastors and ministers are people too, they have struggles just like everyone else. Pride often gets in the way of people seeking help especially in areas of sexual dysfunction. Satan knows how to use this the bring a wedge between marriages, as one person is confused and blaming themselves for not being able to satisfy their spouse, while the spouse is seeking sexual gratification from pornographic sites and sex lines. There are many things which are not taught in a religious setting, but education is power. Many marriages would be saved if people were taught how to connect with each other after marriage. My mother who was born in 1937, has a saying the way you start out in courtship is the way it needs to continue throughout your marriage.

The roses, boxes of candy date nights, should not stop because you say I do. I commend young people who are vested in their marriages and others secluded themselves from other family members to build solidarity in their marriages. This is a good thing. It is difficult for a married woman to run around with her single girlfriends who are always speaking negatively about men. Soon this negative attitude will transfer to the married woman, and she will become critical of her own husband. This also can happen when a married woman befriends a newly divorced woman. The residual effect of her bitterness and brokenness can be transferred to the home of the friend who is emotionally supporting her. One does not often realize that this had occurred until it is too late. A married woman has one purpose and that is how she should please her husband, (sounds old-fashioned right) 1 Corinthians 7:32 -34 Paraphrased the unmarried person is concerns about the Lord's affairs. But in marriage that person is concerned the affairs of the world and how he/ she may please their spouse. They are each concerned with taking care of each other's needs.

The problem is that many women who are single desire to be married but have not explored their singleness in its full context. When they are married, they try to live as single, forgetting that they are married. The winter of 2024, I attended a funeral of an aunt. She lost her husband tragically in an accident during her forties. She never remarried. Instead, she used her singleness to encourage woman of every age, especially widows. She loved her children, grandchildren and great grandchildren and she loved the Lord.

I know a sister in Christ who never married. She used her gift of singleness to provide home to care to babies who were born to mothers who were addicted to crack cocaine. I know another sister who after her divorce devoted herself to the ministry. She became an elder in her church. These women assumed the call to work unto the lord. They viewed their singleness as a gift not a curse. One even chose to be a mother figure when the birth mothers were unable to provide for their children. The gift of charity and hospitality has diminished in our world. No wonder marriages are suffering as well. If we do not have charity in the home love will suffer. The greatest mission field is the home. Ministers and servant leaders are not immune to the spirit of divorce. When there is a lack of communication, respect, and the fear of God in a marriage the seed of divorce can breed in confusion, misunderstanding, frustration anger and rebellion. If you have a tooth ache you would seek relief from a dentist. If you were having chest pains would get to the nearest emergency room. God forbid, you were diagnosed with a terminal illness. You would seek out the best specialist.

So why is it when people are faced with a sign of a termination in their marital relationships, they do nothing to prevent divorce. I understand that there are extenuating circumstances: and will address these later. But when God has called us to peace and the ministry of reconciliation. Why is it so hard to find forgiveness and reconciliation in the body of Christ to save our marriages?

I love scrolling on Facebook and seeing couples who have been married twenty plus years. Those who have been married forty or even 65 years could collaborate in authoring this book.

Modern couples however change their mates faster than they changed out their wardrobes. Is it for lack of discipline understanding or lust. An old pastor may say it is all three.

Love is patient. I do not think anyone married any length of time does not understand this verse.

I love you when you agree with me and when you do not. I love you when you do not clean the room the way I do. I love you even when you forget to take out the trash. I am patient with you when you have just lost your job. I am patient with you when you are recovering from a debilitating illness. I am patient with you when you are working two jobs to support our family. I am patient with you even when you are too tired for our movie night. Love is patient. A few years ago, I met a loving Christian brother in the Lord. He was a family person he had a business and he worked too many hours in the church as he was assistant pastor. Yes, he had a call on his life for ministry. But God convicted him that his first ministry was his family. When I see his Facebook post about his family and children. I know he made the right decision. Parent's if you evolved in seven ministries and you have a family beware. Please reconsider your priorities. God called you to be a husband and father first then a minister of the gospel. Those who were saved in the New Testament the new believers they ministered to their homes first. Then their friends and went into the other parts of the world. The point is they ministered to their families first.

God did not call a married man to forsake his wife and preach the gospel. God is a God of order. The same applies to women. If you are single and in ministry, you do well. If God has called, you to ministry pray about this with your spouse. God will not place a call on you without confirming it by your head (which is your husband). If the two of you are working in ministry together be diligent in the time you spend with each other.

Genisis 2:23 (NASB) The man said "At last this bone of my bones and flesh of my flesh. She shall be called woman, for she was taken out of man. Verse 24 For this reason a man will leave his father and mother and be joined (united) to his wife, and they will become one flesh.

Nothing came before this union which God ordained. Some would say soul mate partner and best friend. We have others who report they just fit together. He reports he found his missing rib. She is bone of my bones and flesh of my flesh.

The Art of being Saved and Single

As I stated before some individuals are blessed to have the gift of singleness and they know that is enough. It is enough because they are complete within themselves and in God. They do not desire marriage to complete their lives. They look to serve God and his people. The most self-sacrificing is well known for loving the unlovable. That is the legacy of the person Mother Theresa

She served her God and the people of India for most of her life. She did not want marriage as would have been the custom in her day but looked to serve God with every ounce of her being. She also may have had doubts of her worthiness to do the task or vision that was set before her. Thankfully, she did not have to deal with social media in her day. The art of comparison can undermine anyone single or married.

The art of being single has do with purpose and living a life that is pleasing to God. Everyone is born with gifts and talents. We are told this in Scripture and if you were fortunate also reinforced by your parents. These gifts have been given to us, to bless the world and our lives. The most confident singles I know are those living out their dreams and walking into their destiny. A few may want marriage at some point in their lives but decide to wait on the direction of God for a suitable mate.

When we speak about suitable, we are speaking of being equally yoke.

How can two walks together unless they agree? If an individual knows this ahead of time it will save much heartache and sleepless nights in the future. You might say well there is a nice guy at my job, and he is single, and it think a Christian. That all sounds great. But if that person is truly a Christian, he will not defile you. He will honor you as a beautiful woman of God and not asks you to do anything that you are uncomfortable doing. I know you may say this sound so old fashioned. Let me give you some examples of woman and men who acted on the flesh and did not seek God.

Sin of Comparison

Sister Precious has been a Christian most of her life. She was raised in the church from her earliest recollection. She went off to college and was able to keep herself pure. She made this vow of purity while she was in high school. She obtained a degree in business and worked extremely hard to start her own company. Precious was doing well as a single woman but started to compare herself and her life with those of her friends who decided to get married and start a family verse going to college. One day Precious met a man through her work. He seems nice and invited her to dinner. He walked her home after the date and kissed her on her cheek. She thought nothing of this. It seemed harmless enough. A few weeks later they had another date and after each date he went ahead to touch a little more. Precious thought that he was truly falling in love with her. When they went on the sixth dated her asked if she had been thinking intimately about him. Precious confessed that she thought about marriage. He promised her a ring if she would sleep with him. The red lights went off but by this time Precious was so in love she did what he asked. The next day she tried to call him, and he would not return her phone call. A few weeks past and still no phone call from the nice guy she met while working. A month later she went to lunch and saw him having lunch and kissing another woman. The incident upset her so much she left works early and sought counseling. Looking back Precious realized they had never prayed together, read the bible together or attended services together. While dating they never discussed marriage or marriage counseling. They only discussed sex. Precious realized that her naivety costed her virginity. She gave her most precious gift away, never to be able to regain it.

The sin of comparison made Sister Precious feel that she was missing out of what life had to offer her. Things might have turned out differently if she had given that desire over to God. Prayer before any decision to change your circumstance is always informed. She went on to obtain counseling and was screened for STD's. It was decided that during the heat of passion she has contacted and STD, she was treated and felt so ashamed of being misled and deceived. (John 10:10) The thief comes to kill steal and destroy) but I came that you might have life and have it more abundantly. Sister Precious reflected before comparing herself to others, she had been contented with her single life. It was the sin of comparison that had led her down a dangerous path. She would recover emotionally and spiritually in time.

Women are not the only ones deceived let look at Brother Bill.

Brother Bill had been widowed two years. He was still attending to his wife's affairs when his friends thought he should get out and meet someone. He had been married 31 years. His wife Elenors clothes were still I the closet. Every now and then he would walk by and sniff her dresses. The fragrance reminded him of her favorite perfume Chanel # 5. He had been meaning to donate her clothes but just could not part with them just yet. It would seem so final, as if she had never existed. Elenors pictures were in every room of the house. He would often have conversations with the pictures in the evening when he was getting off work. He thought about retiring, but what was the use he would just be home all day in an empty house. Bill worked part time and still had his pension coming in as well. Elenore had planned well, and he was financially secure. Working was just a past time for him to be able to see people and interact with the community. They had no children, as their only son was killed in Desert Storm. Bill went to church weekly and attended a men's group twice a month which satisfied Bill. He had a garden which he named after his wife to keep him busy. Bill was adjusting to the single life. He did not wish female companionship. He sought the counsel of his pastor and told him how he was feeling. The pastor agreed that Bill should not be forced into doing something he did not want to do. The pastor, however, did tell him if he wants to start dating to seek guidance and counsel from the Lord. Bill prayed about it and felt that he was not ready to have someone else in his life right now. He waited until he was ready to move on. Two years later he managed to donate his wife clothing to charity. He also packed up all her photographs of her except in his bedroom. Bill started going to activities where single mature women could be found. He went to potluck dinners put on by the church concerts and even joined a Bell choir. He started to meet many women, as women tend to outnumber men in most churches. Bill soon met and red head woman name Janice. Janice looked 20 years younger than her stated age and was a fine figure of a woman. She admitted that she had been married once or twice before but they both died. It seemed like she had the worst luck with her husbands. They all died within seven years of the marriage. Many referred to her as the Black Widow. Janice still worked however as she did not just want to sit at home alone either. Bill and Janice started going out for weekly ice -cream dates. Then progressing to weekly dinners after Sunday service. They dated for about six months and decided that they wanted to look at moving their relationship forward. Bill asked Janice if she would like to speak to the pastor about pre-marital counseling. Jancie replied that she did not believe they needed that because "they each were mature people and could make their own decisions." Bill was torn because he promised the pastor that he would seek counsel before remarriage. Janice told Bill "We know what we want, and we don't need anyone meddling in our affairs." Bill asked Janice if she would sign a prenuptial agreement. Janice replied that also was not necessary as she had her own money and did not need his money. Bill asked Janice to wait a few days and he would give her his decision. Bill prayed and asked God for guidance. Bill reminisced about how things were with Elenore. They prayed together and studied God's word together and attended worship together. Elenore oversaw the household affairs simply fine, But he had faith in his late wife. He had a complete life with Elenore. Although Janice was beautiful, they had no spiritual connections. Bill went to his pastor to tell him about Janice. He had to wait as the police were at the church as well inquiring about Janice. When Bill came in about his concerns, the pastor hung his head down.

Pastor Jim replied" It is strange that you are here today. The police were just hear asking about someone you know. Bill how well do you know Janice? Bill replied" I was here to speak to you about her, I am considering marring her." Pastor Jim" Well I am glad you came her first. Bill I usually do not do this, but you are going to read about it in the newspaper tomorrow. Janice has been indited in the murders of her two late husbands. Bill fell over in his chair" What are you saying?

Pastor Jim" I am saying that Jancie is going to be changed in the deaths of her late husbands!

Bill, "that is why she did not want to come in for premarital counseling. "Wow oh my goodness. Thank you, Lord, for not letting me make a big mistake."

Pastor Jim" Bill are you going to be okay" Bill "I will someday but not today" Excuse me I need to be left alone of a minute."

Bill drove to the cemetery and sat by Elenors grave, "Baby almost messed up today. I really miss you baby! Bill just sat there sobbing and reflecting on his life without Elenor.

Multitude of Counselors

Titus 2: 3 NASB Older women likewise are to be reverent in their behavior, not malicious gossips. Nor enslaved to much wine, teaching what is good. Verse 4 so that they many encourage the younger women to love their husbands, to love their children, to be sensible, pure, workers at home, kind being subject to their own husbands, so that the word of God will not be dishonored.

Church mother's and the missionaries have been the support system of most African- American churches. Educating young women in the walk of salvation and a life to pleasing the Lord. Young women meet with these educators to enhance their church life. Sunday school youth groups and traditional and contemporary services. The church climate changed after Covid 19 and many of the leaders in the church went home to be with the Lord. Leaving a generation that did not have the experiential knowledge of the Lord. One may assume that elderly church women had no knowledge of the world or the sin that tempts younger women. Of- course that could be further from the truth. Just because one is older and is in church now, does not mean that they have always been saved. Elderly women often claim a hard head leads to a soft behind, they are speaking from experience. Such is the case of Mother Beatrice Jackson. She will tell everyone," I have not always been saved. I even black slide once or twice before I committed my life to the Lord. I fell so many times I could not keep count. Then I realized it was not God who was failing me. But I was failing him. When I became reclaimed, my life changed. I started studying the word of God, and not just reading to check off a box every day. I started applying his word to my heart. I began to have dreams and visions of what he needed from me and how I could help the kingdom. It was not just about money. It was about souls. I knew the torment and the vices that they dealt with because God delivered me from my mess. I was a far from the peaceful shore for sure. But he found me and redeemed me, and I am glad about it."

The young women just laughed when they heard her speak not knowing from where she came from or what demons she had dealt with in the past. Soon one young soul would come across her path and then she would realize why Mother Beatrice Jackson had been spared during the pandemic.

Susan a young mother of thirty- three years old with three small children came into the church fellowship shortly after the pandemic. Susan seemed truly repented and was thankful she survived Covid – 19 when others did not include the children's father. They had been married only ten years and she was left to raise three children alone. Mother Beatrice had compassion on the young woman. She became her mentor and confidant. Things were progressing well, when suddenly Susan began to have symptoms that she could not explain. It was found that Susan had kidney disease and would have to go on Dialysis. Susan was on Dialysis for a year when the doctors suggest that she be placed on a transplant list. Susan had no family to speak of since her family and mother were both deceased. She asked members of her fellowship to see if anyone could be a potential match. She knew this was a lot to ask, so she prayed that God would provide a ram in the bush. Mother Beatrice asked friends and family as well to get evaluated to see if anyone was a match. Mother Beatrice had a twin sister and asked her to consider being a kidney donor. She was in excellent condition and always took care of herself. She also was a nurse who knew the importance of kidney donation.

Her sister Barabra, decided to be screened. It was soon discovered that she would be a perfect match for Susan. Interesting information surfaced during typing and cross matching of blood type. Beverly and Susan had similar DNA structures which proved they were related. Beverly was given this information, but Susan was not. Beverly told Beatrice that there was something she wanted to share with her. Beverly told Beatrice that when she went away to college, she became pregnant. No one knew because she never came home that summer from school. She had the baby and placed it up for adoption. She never even looked at the baby girl because she knew if she did, she would have to keep it. Beverly told Beatrice that Susan was her biological daughter. There was silence in the room for a period of ten minutes. Beatrice praised God for the events that brought Susan back into their lives. During the recovery period Beatrice looked at both women sleeping and saw the resemblance.

When Susan awoke both Beatrice and Beverly would be there to share the news with her. It would be a lot to take in, as before surgery she had only Mother Beatrice and a kind donor. When she awoke, she would be greeted by her birth mother and aunt for the first time.

Then surgeon came into the room and announce the transplant was successful. Susan thanked Beverly for her donation, as it meant she would have many more years with her children. Beverly cried and Susan asked if she was all, right? "Are you in pain? I know I am, but it a good kind of pain."

Beverly did not know how to answer that question, Susan I am glad you are going to be all right; you have lovely children. When you are ready, I would like to meet your children once you get home from the Hospital, Susan replied, oh you have already done so much.

Beverly replied, Susan this is just the beginning of what God is going to do for you.

Barbara later came into the room and noticed that Beverly was holding Susan's hand. Beverly said I will tell her when it is time. Let her sleep for now. She has a long road to recovery.

Beverly continued to watch over Susan during her recovery period. Six months later Susan was functioning well. She no longer needed dialysis or any of the earlier medication. She was however taking the medication that would help her from rejecting the kidney. As Susan transitioned to her daily activities, Beverly thought it was time for the talk. It occurred on one sunny day in the early spring. Beverly had come to visit and bring the grandchildren chocolate chip cookies which she made that morning. While the two women were sipping tea and sharing a chocolate chip cookie. Beverly asked Susan about her birth mother. Susan thought this was a strange way to start a conversation, but she acknowledged the request for information, as she owned her very life to Beverly. Susan replied" I really do not know very much about her. You see she gave me up, as she was a student in college. Her family did not even know she had a baby. I am certain if they knew, my grandparents might have raised me. All I know is that she left me to pursue her own dreams.

Beverly started to cry upon hearing the information. "I am sorry that your life has left you with so many questions. You are a wonderful person and mother to your children. Susan, I want you to understand. That your birth mom had no support and did what she felt was best for you. As you are aware that was a different time. Things are different now. There is no stigma from being an unwed mother. Women are choosing to have children whether they are married or not.

Susan replied "you are right. It was a different time. It is never easy being a single other no matter what your earlier status may have been."

The Voice of Experience

I understand what Susan is saying: What little girl when she was growing up said when I grow up, I want to become a single mom? That would be ludicrous. One chooses of not be a single mom as a matter of personal conviction. Married divorced or single. The death of her husband left her to raise their children alone. Women who were raped abused and could not give themselves over to the abortion procedure, as it would also traumatize them related to their pro-life stance. Suffered the same fate. But for whatever reason, no girl at age nine or ten, said themselves when I grow- up I want to be a single mom!

This is especially true if they were raised by a single mother and witness her struggles to put food on the table or to pay the mortgage.

Beverly could not bring herself to have the talk that day with Susan. It would have to wait for a more opportune time. Susan had enough to contended with recuperating and being a single mother.

A Mariage of Convenience

Sally Sue was 38 years old when she met her daddy Warbucks. He was settling into middle age and felt that Sally was a catch. He had recently divorced second wife. Sally as a blue-eyed bombshell that reminded him of Marilyn Monroe. She was curvy in all the right places which made him feel ten feet tall. Daddy Warbucks (Steve) was greying around the temples with a salt and pepper beard. He had a generous belly, but Sally called him her teddy bear. They met at a local dance hall that catered to country music and the local farm hands. Neither Sally or Steve was religious and lived for today. That was their motto. They had three months of fast dating and one month where they discussed living together. And as time would have it during month five, they went to the courthouse to get married. They had no premarital counseling. A few months later Steve was diagnosis, with colon cancer. Sally hung around for three months until he was diagnosed as being terminal. She left in her red 1986 Corvette in the middle of the night and left Steve a Dear John letter. The marriage of convenience had served it is time and Sally moved onto to greener pastures. Steve would spend his remaining time at the house in the presence of strangers all because of a marriage of convenience.

Lust of the Flesh

Men are not the only ones who can be tricked by the enemy, when it comes to quick and easy marriages. Women who find themselves suddenly widowed or divorced can be easy prey for the right opportunist. A person of interest looking for a woman with means who can take care of him. She appears hurt vulnerable and in need of emotional comfort. She may appear forgetful or scatter brain due to the shock of her status. It has yet to sink in that she now is single. Not by choice but by circumstances. The problem is that she was once a married woman. Her physical and emotional needs were met by her husband. The man who is no longer there. She wanders each day fragile, tearful and on the verge of making the biggest mistake of her life. (It is amazing how many people show up at the funeral. A week later one can vaguely find a soul who will lend a kind ear of compassion). And so it is that our widow is to navigate the waters of singleness alone and without a proper guide. It has been 20 years since she dated anyone. The last person she dated was her late husband. Who would help her to navigate this new life with understanding and compassion?

Singles groups are helpful, but the need to speak to someone daily can be dauting.

Few people understand the problematic situation that the newly divorced or widow face. The longing to have a sincere relationship often escapes those who find themselves in this situation. One's history can also complicate things when one looks to please God in all their relationships. Women who want to live Godly lives are often at risk for meeting opportunist and solacious men. It is for this reason that many single women are celibate. Christian and non- Christian alike. They avoid the trauma and the discouraging relationships that can lead to self-doubt and a compromised lifestyle.

Marriage Not an Option

Matron Richardson a Caucasian raised in the Jim Crow south, and one of the first women truck drivers in America. She was raised having a Black housekeeper. Although politically incorrect Negro that was the terminology used in the 1940's. The elderly lady said her housekeeper was more like family. This situation taught her a lot about race relations. Matron Contance Richardson married a man from the south who was as respectable drunk. The only thing he had going for him was that he was white and goodlooking. He could not keep a job. She had five children for him, but since he was unable to keep a job, she started driving his truck to keep a roof over her family's head. She was southern through and through. Yes, she also was a strong and powerful woman who had dealt with a drunken solacious- spouse. Constance did not believe in divorce, so she separated from her husband and remained single all the days of her life, even after his death. I asked her why she never remarried after his death?

"Lady after what I have been through, I would not have a man if his backside were rimmed in in gold and diamonds. And if any man would every approach me, I have those brass knuckles over there to show him not to mess with me."

Mrs. Contance Richardson married before the age of premarital counseling. She was instructed by her family to marry a gentleman in her community one of her families choosing. She had little choice in the matter. This was a different time, 1927 to be exact. Today women have choices to marry or remain single. There are some who possess the gift of singleness.

The art of being single has do with purpose and living a life that is pleasing to God. Everyone is born with gifts and talents. We are told this in Scripture, and if you were fortunate also to have those gifts reinforced by your parents, you were blessed. These gifts have been given to us, to bless the world and our lives. The most confident singles I know are those living out their dreams and walking into their destiny.

As I stated before some individuals are blessed to have the gift of singleness and they know that is enough. It is enough because they are complete. There are those who have the gift of singleness and should be aware that this is a gift from God. Whether they have never been married, are widowed, or divorced, this singleness however it came to be is a gift to be cherished within themselves and in the Lord. They do not do desire marriage to complete their lives. They look to serve God and live a full and complete live outside of marriage.

Service To God

One may ask how does one serve God? The most complete answer is to know God, so that you may serve him doing what he has placed in your heart to do. Service to God is not wrapped in how many times a week you are found sitting in a place of worship. Nor it is found in how much you give to a local assembly, but in your service to God's creation.

You may ask how is this related to the Marriage covenant? Let us look to scripture to answer this question.

1 Corinthians 7:3-6 9 NASB Speaks of the duties of husbands and wives to ministering to one another, physically emotionally and spiritually.

When reflecting on the many married couples that I both saw and spoke with, a prevalent theme prevailed. I married my best friend. These couples have more than just a physical attraction they have a soul bond. I stated earlier that some endured test and trials before they were married. One case comes to mind, where the bride was taking care of her mother who was diagnosed with dementia. The groom understood his bride's commitment to her mother and joined in caring for the mother. The couple even started a nursing home ministry so that his wife could remain close to her mother and the care she was receiving at the nursing home. The couple remained resolute in their love for each other and the love of the wife's mother. The marriage covenant goes far beyond physical beauty. It transcends the boundaries of selflessness and self- gratification. Couples who are united in love and covenant work through difficulty time with grace and compassion for each other.

Sickness and disease can bring out the worse in those who are afflicted by it as well as those who are caring for their spouse. A spouse who is going through treatment for cancer knows this too well. One not only loses their hair and a substantial amount of weight, but one's self esteem may be crushed in the process. Let us face it we all would love to always look our best. Yet, when illness strikes this is not the case. Love is patient and kind in all situations. (When I worked as a nurse, I saw the best and the worse in people taking care of their spouses. I did not have to venture off too far to figure out who had taken their covenant seriously). One young couple comes to mind many years ago. I was working on the Oncology ward. A young couple just married a week ago was on the ward. I found it strange that the young wife was sleeping in the same bed as her husband, until I learned that they were just married. They were spending their honeymoon on the Oncology ward. They had found out during a routine blood test before the wedding that the young man had Leukemia.

Treatments forty years ago are not what they are today. The rounds of Chemotherapy quickly compromised his fragile immune system. The young wife stayed by his side morning and night. Unfortunately, the young man developed a GI Bleed that could not be controlled. He was taken to surgery but died on the table. My heart went out to the young woman she was married and widowed in the same month.

This young woman showed the kind of love that endures despite a medical diagnosis. She could have walked away once she realized that her soon to be husband had an incurable illness. She chose to stay. No matter the cost. I will never forget her wailing and screams of agony once she realized he had died in surgery. Her plans dissipated. I did learn later that before the young man underwent for treatment the disease. He banked his sperm so that they would be able to have children. I cannot say for certain that his plans were successful. I know only that they loved each other regardless of his medical condition.

1Corinthians13:13 NASB But now faith, hope and love remain, these three, but the greatest of these is love.

Beware of Distractions

Marriage is a life event. Many couples will spend decades together building families and businesses. Some couples even leave that legacy to the next generation. Couples can be faced with many distractions that can lead to confusion and frustration if they are not careful. Family members and friends no matter how well- meaning can often disrupt the harmony in a couple's life. They do not mean to interrupt the flow of matrimonial bliss, but they often interrupt the couple's life with their own personal baggage and agenda on the unsuspecting couple. Before you know it, the couple is arguing over someone is else 's poor decision making I love the country saying "Stay in your own lane ". If said another way, it is not my business what goes on in other people's lives. You may say, that is not very Christian, so let me explain.

Henrietta was a young widow. She was ill prepared to be left alone at the age of thirty when her husband died suddenly in an accident. She struggled for a while but when she received the settlement from the insurance company, she did not know what or how to manage the increase of fiscal responsibility. You see Henrietta, always had a giving spirit. She would send money aboard fostering Child Aid societies, as well as supporting her church. She also gave a handout to everyone in need. She moved in with her adult children after settling her husband's estate. They were surprised to discover that she had given away a small fortune. She barely had enough to live out the rest of her days with her small pension. Although giving of itself it not a terrible thing, Henerietta, had not used discernment in giving away her inheritance. She had zeal without knowledge about her future. She made everyone's problem hers alone to solve. (Listen carefully to this make no major discissions in regards finances at least two years after you have experienced a death or divorce). Many individuals have been taken advantage of in situations after the death of a spouse. Unfortunately, those interlopers are there, and they will attack any prey within their sight.

Those who have been divorced can face a similar fate if not managing their child support and alimony carefully after a divorce. It would be a wise decision to place finances in a trust for children or even later for yourself after the emotional effects of the divorce or death dissipates.

James 1:27 NASB- This is pure religion in the sight of our God and Father, to visit orphans and widows in their distress, and to keep oneself unstained by the world.

I am applauded to know that some individuals without discernment would try to take advantage of a widow or widower when that are most fragile and wounded. God have mercy on us and let us show compassion, and not seek our own self gain. There are those void of understanding or compassion where financial gain is concerned.

Genesis 2:24 (NASB) For this cause a man shall leave his father and mother and shall cleave to his wife: and be joined to his wife: and they shall become one flesh. This one sentence has so much revelation in it.

Its speaking of spiritual and intimate relationships. Not only the joining one flesh intimately but intertwined as to know the needs of their spouse. The sensitivity in marriage can be compromised by those who are allowed to negatively change the relationship. It speaks of parents, but it could also be siblings, friends and former or past acquaintances. (Watching the company, you keep it key in supporting a healthy relationship. One does not spend so much time with his friends that he neglects' his household and his wife.

My mother always said whatever you did to get her you need to do that and more to keep her. A couple who has a continual dating life and intimate time together will be able to keep their relationship intact. It is also advisable that they are on the same page spiritually. A couple who prays together, worships together and studies Gods word together can stand up to the attacks of the enemy. There is not one couple that I have known or met that has not gone through trials in their marriage. Faith and prayer and a spiritually inner circle who holds covenant as sacred will help them in the time of trials.

Sins of the Flesh

It is always sad to hear of infidelity in a marriage. Nothing could be more painful for either spouse. It fractures the trust and love that was built -up over time.

Feelings of anger betrayal and abandonment are some of the surface feelings that appear. He or she no longer feels validated and loved. The first inclination is to move away from the person who hurt you. A separation or cooling off period to see if there is anything of value that still is after the act of infidelity. Everyone deals with this differently, Depression and thoughts of self-harm or harming the person that hurt you are common. Sometimes it is better to have some distance to gain perspective after you have had time to cool off. Can a marriage survive after the act of infidelity?

Counseling and communication on the problems which led up to the act may help to heal the wounds. But will the other party be able to forgive their spouse, and will the offending party be able to forgive themselves for hurting his partner in that way? These are questions that can only be answered in time and with counseling and much prayer.

Gambling

This form of idolatry has claimed many marriages. Homes and families have been lost to the lust for more than one could afford. They used to call it "Keeping up with the Joneses."

The lust of the eyes the lust of the flesh and the pride of life. 1John 2:16 (NASB).

Let me tell you about Wayne and Karen. They met in church and had a whirl wind romance. He was less educated than she but that did not seem to bother her at first. He later went on to get his CDL license. He was gone most of the time, He told his wife that he was making good money, but when he returned home, he had little to show for it. Wayne sold some property before they were married but that money also disappeared before Karen could count it as an asset. Karen became suspicious and confronted Wayne. He admitted that he was going to the Slots in his free time.

Karen said they needed to go to counseling so that they could save their marriage. Wayne went reluctantly and denied he had a problem. The counselor at the end of the session told Karen, as Wayne had walked out before the session ended. The only hope he saw for the couple was divorce. If Karen did not leave the marriage Wayne would Bankrupt her. Wayne had also maxed out Karen's credit cards playing the slots. Karen was stubborn and wanted so desperately to save her marriage. But it was too late. She filed for the divorce and shortly afterwards Bankruptcy. She had lost everything because her husband held on to his idol. Later Karen after going through counseling realized that she enabled Wayne in his gambling because she took care of everything. Karen also found out later that Wayne also had an addiction to pornography. Karen felt betrayed and worthless. This new state of being divorced and destitute left her feeling less than a woman. Worse than that It had her questioning her ability to her from God.

Mental illness and Addictions

Marriage can be complicated when one or both parties has a mental illness or addition. Unfortunately, an individual may have both. The untreated mental illness may cause marital discord when the patient is prescribed medication and refuses to take the prescribed medicated and seeks relief from street drugs and alcohol. The addiction is usually not discovered until later in the marriage. The spouse may suspect that their partner drinks a little too much or stays out too much at night partying. The discovery of the problem may present itself through credit card debit, loans and bounced checks. The revelation discovered by the sober party, causes anger frustration and seeking a resolution. Physical and mental abuse often manifest through the addicted person. Expecting a person to stay married under this circumstance is unreasonable, especially if the life of a family member is at stake. Substance abuse counseling is often sought before mental health counseling to alleviate the substance abuse.

Marriage is challenging under normal circumstance of life but, when addictions and mental illness present themselves, sanity is a daily battle. The sober spouse needs much understanding, counseling and possible a safety plan to go on with their life.

Abuse

Why would this be included in a book on marriage? I felt like it should be addressed as some women even in Christian circles have been physically emotional and physically abused by their spouses. I was walking with a dear friend some years ago who shared with me a story that not only broken my heart but caused anger to rise within me. She sharded about a docile woman who was being abused by her husband. When the woman reported this to the church elder. He laid blame on the wife and told her if you were more submissive your husband would not have beaten you. The woman wanted to be an obedient wife. So, she went back to her abusive spouse. The next week she was beaten so badly that she had four broken ribs. While she recovered, she left that church and went to a secure location. She could no longer tolerate the beating and felt misled and abuse by her church for not standing up for her as a woman. It should be said that submission goes both ways in marriage, and beating is not a part of submission. The spouses submit to each other as to God. One who loves his own body would never abuse it. One who loves his wife as he does his own body would never abuse her.

The Calling of Marriage

Now this may surprise you, but there are those who have been called to marriage. They were not just physically attracted to someone but called to be a spouse to a specific individual. They were called to marriage much like a vocation. Last year I attended the funeral of a dear cousin. The service was a momentous occasion celebrating her life. But what stood out to me, was that she was called to be a wife. Not only a wife but a minister's wife. They were married 39 years. During the ceremony, her husband explained how she would leave his food at his mother's house, or how she would iron his clothes before they were married. How she would come by and clean his room. Some may say she was claiming her territory. But she knew who she was and who she was called to be. The wife of a minister. One might say that she had an anointing on her to do the work of marriage and family. As I further listened to the family explain how she created things for each of her children to commemorate milestones in their life. I needed to further convincing that she was called to the work of marriage and family. She was faithful until her death.

This is also true of men who are called to be husbands. They are above else great providers but Godly men. They see their lives as a devotion to God and their families. Years ago, I did not know this was possible until I met one such individual for myself. He embodied the marriage covenant. I never met a more earnest diligent individual in my entire life. God and family was always first. He valued his wife beyond all else. His life revolved around his wife. They were married later in life. Still, one would think that they had been married for decades as they were so connected with each other. His every thought was how to make a better life for his wife. She anticipated his every need and desire. They discovered later in life that they had been called to the ministry of marriage and marriage reconciliation.

My mother always said whatever you did to get her you need to do that and more to keep her. A couple who has a continual dating life and intimate time together will be able to support their relationship. It is also advisable that they are on the same page spiritually. A couple who prays together, worships together and studies Gods word together can stand up to the attacks of the enemy. They are committed the ministry of marriage.

It takes work.

I am surprised that even though one is called to ministry they feel that they should not work at it. The same applies to marriage one must consciously work at being sensitive to the spirit and the needs of their spouse. A habit my husband and I developed before we married was to study and pray together. We felt if we could keep God at the center of our relationship, even when we missed the mark, he would get us back on track.

The times of disconnectedness came when we did not seek God's presence or let others distract us from our marriage commitment. If you were to think of marriage as one thinks of ministry, then you will start to get the picture of God's plan for his family. Loving God and loving God's people may seem easier said than living it out. It is amazing how differently we view marriage after the pomp and circumstance of the celebration is over. Life goes on bills come and go and trials never take a vacation. Knowing that your covenant is strong is how you weather the storms of life. I find it impressive that our parents married in times of economic stress and managed to have fruitful and productive marriages. I remember my, mother telling me how the ladies of the church catered her wedding. The women of the church came together to make sure she had a nice wedding as her father was no longer living and her mother did not work outside of the home once they left the farm. In 1956 they had a modest wedding, but their marriage thrived until his death. They did not have a 40-thousand-dollar wedding, but they had love in Christ and each other. Marriage ministry as it should be called as one ministers to their spouse in marriage. This is not once a week. But daily ministering to the needs of each other. I am not speaking about one-sided submission but the couple ministers to each other during their lifetime together as husband and wife.

The husband is not more than the wife nor the wife more than the husband. They serve each other in submission as unto God. Service is easy when the partner is beautiful healthy and is good spirits. What happens when the reverse happens? What if one spouse develops cancer and must go through treatment. What if they lost their hair figure and became a shadow of their prior self?

What if they have lost their job and fall into depression, feeling worthless and hopeless? What happens if they are accused of a crime and sentenced to prison? Yes, I know these are difficult circumstances. These may be puzzling questions but life happens to us all.

What happens to the covenant under these circumstances?

1 Corinthians 13:7 NASB It keeps every confidence, it believes all things, hopes all things, endures all things.

Verse 13: NASB But now abides faith, hope and love remain, these three: but the greatest of these is love.

For some this may sound like a fairy tale. Again, I emphasize that marriage is work. There might be days it just flows and there is perfect harmony. There might be days that there is bitterness and anger, and one must look quickly to rectify such feelings. Find out what the problem is and address it. There is nothing the enemy likes better than to destroy the homes of God's children.

Doing your Homework

It is important to adhere to this bit of advice. I know couples who have taken their health seriously and worked on losing weight together. As they look to be better for themselves and their spouses. They have learned what taking care of the temple of God really means. We all have seen television shows that depict older married couples as dumpy men or women who have let themselves go. The spouse becomes discouraged and seeks out a different love interest to feel attractive again. This is a distraction of the enemy, but the warning is clear. Couples need to support their health for themselves as well as their spouse. Gaining one hundred pounds over the course of a marriage is not healthy for you or your spouse. Learning to be discipline in all things, especially in gluttony. This one vice has ended many marriages. Why is it that we can claim victory over every sin except the sin of gluttony? Knowing that physical attraction as well as emotional attraction brought the couple together. Why would anyone want to make gluttony their idol? This is a distraction in their marriage. When one chooses to make gluttony their god, it is replacing what the person feels is missing from the marital relationship. Depression can also cause a change in the persons appetite. A lack of dissatisfaction in marriage will cause an increase in weight. An individual may also compensate lack of intimacy with eating.

Gluttony substance abuse, pornography, sexual addictions all destroy the marriage relationship. A lack in dissatisfaction with life as much as marriage may be the cause for unhappiness in the life of the person. We know that all sin is sin regardless how it manifests itself. These sins destroy the temple of the living God.

1Corinthians3:16 NASB- Do you not know that you are a temple of God, and that the Spirit of God dwells in you? (Some version reference temples of the Living God)

It is important that couples continue to persevere in prayer and in fellowship with one another to quench the fiery darts of the devil. There may be a time where professional counseling is advisable to keep the marriage intact.

Counseling at one time was dispelled by those called believers believing that they should be able to manage anything on their own and with God's word. This is true as far as the interpretation is understood. But with all your getting obtain an understanding.

Proverbs19:20 NASB- Listen to advice and accept discipline, so that you may be wise the rest of your days. It surprising to me how often we tear down the works of our own hands with the words of our mouths.

If we consider the proverb that life and death is in the power of the tongue, then why do so many believers choose to curse their marriages before they are well into their covenant? Proverbs 18:21 NASB.

A person who intentional chooses to speak Life into their marriage will reap the fruits of what they speak into the atmosphere.

I met a dear sister. No matter what it looked like she continued to speak life into her marriage. She was a Pentecostal by family association and became Baptist in her adult years. She married a catholic. They were married for 58 years, three weeks before he died, he gave his life to the Lord. She did not bagger him nor tell him where he was wrong. She let her light shine as to bring her husband to the Lord.

Sealed Unto the Day of Redemption

Ephesians 4:30 NASB, do not grieve the Holy Spirit of God, by whom you were sealed for the day of redemption. I would like you to consider this verse in the context of marriage. How can we grieve the <u>Holy Spirit in marriage? I am so glad you asked this question. This passage of scripture refers to our</u> life in Christ and the putting off the former life. The works of the flesh grieve the Holy Spirit. In verse 31-32. It states: Let all bitterness and wrath and anger and clamor and slander be put away from you along with malice. Verse 32, and be kind to one another, tender hearted, forgiving each other, just as God in Christ also has forgiven you.

This verse hits marriage right where we live. When it comes to our covenant partner should we not employ the Holy Spirit to helps us in this as well. When we fail to do so our seal's leak.

God showed me this while I was cleaning up the kitchen one morning. That is how he speaks to me in the everyday things of life. I was busy cleaning the kitchen. When I notice a black band on the counter but paid it no mind. I saw my new tumble and attempted place the lid on the tumbler and it just moved around. I thought I needed to apply pressure to it, but it still would not hold. It was not until I remembered the seal, that the tumbler became useful again. God said to me that the problem. They have forgotten to seal their marriages.

This is why bitterness, wrath, anger, frustration miscommunications and isolation take place in marriages. The seal of love peace and patience has been broken in many marriages. Couples instead of securing the seal, get involved in all kinds of distractions which pull them away from their marriages. This puts stress on the seal until it eventually becomes dilapidated.

Remember that lid I spoke about and it not fitting properly. I thought at first, I needed to apply pressure to make it fit. Sadly, some of us when our marriages are not working, we apply force or pressure to the circumstances. If not careful when can do irreputable damage to a fragile situation, which usually just makes matters worse.

The husband is not more than the wife nor the wife more than the husband. They serve each other in submission as unto God. This is ministry to God in your marriage. Honoring him in all things. Let us walk together in unity.

Breathing Life into Your Marriage

Momma said how you start out is how you will end up.

My mother always said whatever you did to get her you need to do that and more to keep her. A couple who has a continual dating life and intimate time together will be able to support their relationship. Long walks enhance communication. Getting rid of all distractions, I mean all. Signing off Facebook for a weekend to concentrate on your person, while putting your cell phones on do not disturb. Warm showers together or soaking in hot tubs together. I know of a couple that takes frequent get weekend get aways. It is their way of saying that we matter to one another. If you find that you are financial unable to get away, try doing a project together. Gardening and landscaping can be quiet satisfying when done together. Try cooking a meal together. You will have a sense of accomplishment and togetherness. I find it amazing that when I block out the noise, I can hear from God fully and know how to minster to my husband.

When together try to stay away from any words that bring death into your marriage. Words like I am devastated, or I am I a state of dissonance. I feel distant from you or that we are in a state of disorder, or I feel like I am dying when I am with you. I am not telling you to deny your feelings. But there is a way to tell her spouse that you love them want to strengthen your marriage without tearing them apart.

Always start off by telling your spouse what they mean to you. Their qualities that you admire and how you want to strengthen your marriage. Affirm them for who they are not for what you want to change. Reminded them of how you felt the day you married them and what you have accomplished together. Let them know that you long to have quality time with them, so that you can do some of the things you once did before life happened. Loving words build the bridge over any bog in your relationship. My husband when he wants to get my attention calls me "Lovely" other loving terms Baby, Queen, Beauty." A loving husband will always have an enduring term for this wife. Woman may refer to their husbands as their "Boaz, Protector, Loving King." Affirmation is key to any marriage. Each morning and every night a couple should affirm one another. You are each other's gift from the Lord. When affirming your spouse, remind them how desirable they are to you. Some men tell their wives every time I see you, I just want to kiss those lips or reach out and hug you. I am so glad you are mine. That is what I call building the fire. There is no telling what will happen after that. But I am sure they both will be pleased.

When my husband first met me, he would walk by my office and stare at me. I asked him "What are you starting at?" He replied "the most beautiful industrious woman I have even met. I admire you so much." He continues to affirm me each day. It does not matter how many birthdays we have shared together. I am still his "Lovely" My husband told me the something so special the other day it made me smile every time I thought of it.

He said "I always wanted to have you in my pocket so I can take you everywhere I go. And now I can." He pulled out his cell phone an showed me a picture of myself looking as I say quiet fetching. I was glowing on the picture because of his love. I was proud to be the object of his love and admiration after all these years.

When I met my husband, I was a struggling student and nurse working my way through graduate school. He was my best friend and a great supported and encourager of my goals. He read all my term papers and my final project. When I told him I was going to graduate he asked me where and when? He went right with me. My middle daughter also went with me. They both said how proud they were of me for completing my goals. Later that year my husband asked me to marry him. We were married two years later. Marriage this time for me meant something different. I had never been treated like a queen before, yet when I married may husband, I became his queen. He made certain that he was going to be a good provider. He has been there right by my side every step of the way. He did not assume that I would stop working because that is what he admired about me. He encouraged me to do whatever the Lord placed in my heart to do. He continues to do whatever he can to breathe life into our marriage and I do the same. Knowing that the enemy would attempt to destroy what God has joined together. Which is why we fight in prayer every day and thank God for the gift we have in each other!

I recall my mother telling me that when my parents were married, they moved to Ohio a year later. My father felt that God had a work for him to do there. What I find interesting is that my parents left the home of their family of origin much like Abram and Sari to go to a city they knew little about to start their new life! They left the past behind them the familiar for the unfamiliar. This is a lesson in togetherness and seeking God for the future of your home and protecting your spouse even from well-meaning family members. This is difficult for wives at times because we want to be close to our families. But the scripture states what God has joined together let no man divide or cause division between husband and wife.

Historically different sects of Black church in the past have been a source of separating husband and wives. This is especially true if the wife became a Christian after she married her husband. The husband not understanding the wife's devotion to God. May feel threatened by another man (the preacher) thinking that the wife will run off with the preacher. As she is spending so much time at the church. This is a confusing time in the home of a woman who has recently given her life to the Lord. She wants to please her husband, but feels pulled to please the Lord, the church, and the membership. You can see how this might cause discord in the home. Unfortunately, even couples who served the Lord together often find themselves living a life out of balance. As one becomes a believer it should enhance the home life does not tear it apart.

1 Peter 3:1- 2 NASB In the same way, you wives, be subject to your own husbands so that even if any of them are disobedient to the word, they may be won over without a word by the behavior of their wives, as they observe your pure and respectful behaviors. This reminds me of that dear sister who prayed for her husband to accept the lord. She never brow beat him but showed the Love of God to him. While he was at home, in bed one day he called her to himself. He had been watching Chales Stanley on the television. He reported to her that he had accepted the Lord as his savior. They had been married for 53 years. What a marvelous testimony of her faith and perseverance in the Lord!

A Well-Watered Garden

I love creation and plant life. I have plants inside my home and all around my home. I have three gardens. No, I do not live on twenty acres of land, but we make do. The thing about all my plants and gardens is that my husband planted them. I was speaking to an old friend who was once a source of comfort before my husband, and I started dating. (I no longer speak to him). I told him about this gentleman that I met who said he would plant me a garden because I was used to having one in my previous residence. When I told the old fella that my new friend was planting me a garden.

He paused and said "Wait, that man is planting you a garden!

How long have you known him? I said about six months. He paused again and said wholly. If this man is planting, you a garden this must be your husband." Well shut the door! I was standing there holding the phone while speaking with this guy who just proclaimed that the man planting my garden was going to be my husband. Two years later it happened. I am amazed just how closes one door and opens another. I was not thinking of starting a new relationship. I was still mourning the loss of the past. But God, in his timing saw to it that all things happened as it was predestined.

Isaiah 58:11 NASB - And the Lord will continually guide. And shall satisfy your desire in scorched places and give strength to your bones: and you shall be like a well-watered garden, and like a spring of water whose waters do not fail.

When I met my husband then friend I was like a scorched land. Beaten by life and circumstances. Yes, I had lost hope in ever marrying again, ever marrying again. I had buried two husbands, even the one I had divorced and remarried. I just wanted to take care of my younger children and finish graduate school. When I relocated to take care of my mother, I had idea what God had in store for me. As I said marriage was the last thing on my mind. I worked six jobs in the first year to provide for my family and continue my education.

I worked long hours sometimes 18 hours as a nurse due to staff shortages and continued with my education. This is what my co-worker witnessed when he met me. So, when he called me industrious, I knew what he meant. He just did not understand how much I wanted to complete my education. I later found out that he worked as hard as I did between counseling and teaching college courses. How we ever found time to date is beyond me? He became my friend and confidant, and I became his cook and nurse. Later after marriage I would still be his cook and nurse in a more loving way. I am honored to be that for him.

I calculated between my husband and myself that we have 53 years of marriage experience together. All that experience was not good but proved profitable in our later years. I prophesied to my husband when I met him that God would make is later years better than his former years. God is Faithful. He has done exactly what he said he would do!

My mother always said whatever you did to get her you need to do that and more to keep her. A couple who has a continual dating life and intimate time together will be able to sustain their relationship.

Our first date together was to a movie (my husband up until his time had never been to a movie in America). Our second date was bowling. (He had never been bowling before meeting me). These first helped lay the groundwork for the coming years of our lives. We took a lot of first trips to new and exciting places that neither of us had ever been.

These first helped us to keep our marriage new and exciting. It did not matter if it was a cruise or discovering a new hiking trail in an unknown forest. The point is we were together for some much-needed alone time away from all the distractions. How many first can you say that you have had with your spouse? The biggest complaint I hear with couples is that they just outgrew one another. Do not let this happen to you. You have the power to control this. Speak life into your marriage and not death.

This concept is true no matter demographics from which you may come. I am aware that couples who share the same religious perspective and place God first in their marriages see their marriages as a ministry to each other and their families.

I have spoken to many couples of varies races and ethnicities. The focus is always on the wife and family. When one loses that perspective, we give room for the adversary. Ministry starts at home.

I am certain you may have heard of the Proverbs 31 woman. I am certain that she is the most excellent wife because her husband equipped her to be just that. He did not see her capabilities as competition but something to be admired and cultivated. She is industrious, futuristic in her outlooks as well as her opportunities to better her family's condition. Soloman states this in Prov 31:29-31 "Many any daughters have done nobly, but you have excelled them all. Charm is deceitful and beauty is vain, but a woman who fears the Lord, she shall be praised. Give her the product of her hands, and let her works praise her in the gates."

This woman had vision for her herself and her family. May we do likewise and cast our vision on the fruitful produce of our words, and actions towards building up our families.

The question remains is the marriage covenant extinct. Those who have longevity in marriage will tell you that the covenant is alive and well. Just as the spirit moved upon the face of the waters, it can move upon marriages and homes in this dispensation.

As I author this book I pray for a revival of marriage commitment. I took a course recently that shocked me, and which prompted me to author this book. The course informed that couples are granted now a no-fault divorce all over this country with little or no provocation. God had been dealing with me about marriages for two years. I have met with and prayed with many women who were in the valley of decision concerning their marriages. I wish I could say all have been saved. The ones who were headed for divorce never sought counseling. Whether it be in the church or out of the church. This caused much heart ache to both parties. Lives had been changed with the stroke of a pen.

We know that there is no one righteous but the Lord. It is through his power and might that we live victorious. We can claim this for our marriages. It not only covers salvation, but the entirety of our lives. He came that we might have life and that to the full in every area of our lives.

Single Again

My first husband died as result of a motorcycle accident. While he was at home recuperating, he asked me to go to the store to pick up some mixed nuts. When I returned home, he was struggling to breath. I prayed and called the ambulance. He arrested in the ambulance they attempt to revive him three times. An autopsy was performed he had a pulmonary embolism that blocked the return of blood his heart. When he died, he was thirty-six and I was twenty-nine years old. Although I had been warned that my husband would die, I did not want to accept it. I was raw emotionally for six months. During that time, I made some horrible decisions with finances and relationships, out of grief and confusion. I really wanted my husband back. He was saved and had just dedicated himself to the lord. I could have used an intercessory prayer team around me then. Most people saw me as a young widow with an inheritance. They did not realize how painful the experience of walking through life alone without my best friend was for me. My daughter Darlene Dues also suffered from the loss of her father, but I could not see it at the time. It took me two years to emotional get on my feet. Not for lack of attention but that I was attracting the wrong attention. I want to share with you some insights that I have gained living the single life after death of a spouse or divorce. A state of shock and disbelief is what one experiences. This occurs when the death is sudden or anticipated. The situation of divorce for many is like a death, but with the residual effects of running into the ex-spouse in periodic encounters. I want to speak about the struggles and merits of each position. The first time I was widowed, the Lord forewarned me. My then spouse had just been in a traffic accident. He was riding to work on a motorcycle which he previously had purchased a few days earlier. A drunk driver hit him. He laid in the street a while before being taken to the hospital. At the time of the accident neither of us had cell phones. It was a different time. He spent a week in the hospital and came home to recover. As I was preparing the house for his arrival, I had a strong presence of intercession that came upon me. The voice of the Lord told me six weeks and I would be a widow. I tried to shake that off, but it persisted, and I prayed through that revelation in sorrow. When my husband came home, he was a different man. He even wanted to go to church with me after the accident. The night before he died, he told me that he had a vision of heaven. The next day he sent me to the store to buy a can of mixed nuts.

I never took the young widow's class, not that there was such a thing at that time. I had no one to guide me on my journey, I had to figure it out through trial and error. Honestly, there were a lot of errors. I was traveling down a road that I had never been before and had no instruction on what to expect. I made a lot of poor decisions based on emotion. Remember I previously said that you should not make any major decision for at least two years after a loss. If I had followed that advice, I would be a lot richer for it today. A person who is amid emotional and spiritual turmoil should be carefully supported through the life transition. The behavioral sciences instruct us that major life transitions can negatively impact one's mental health. Many people did not take mental health as seriously as they do today. How many widows could have benefited from a good therapist after the loss of a spouse?

Certainly, even those who are divorced often need the same emotional support as a widow, after the divorce. Individuals often hide from family and friends as they are embarrassed and feel isolated after the divorce. One such person told me that they felt as they were losing their mind. They no longer could claim the married status and really did not know who they were as a person. One's identity shifts and changes as does one's perspective of how they fit in the world with this new status.

A new identity brings in new opportunity. I returned to college l to complete by bachelor's degree after my husband died. I was single for those years and focused on working and going to college. That gave me a new appreciation for myself that I completed something I had previously put off. The experiences of- course expanded my horizons. Shortly after Graduation I married again. My life was changing for the better. I was surprised that six months after marriage to find out I was pregnant. That may seem normal to you, but it was a surprise to both my husband and me. You see when I was a younger woman, I was told that it would be difficult for me to conceive related to PCOS. Poly Cystic Ovary Disease. My oldest daughter at the time I conceived was 13 years of age. But God, in his grand design allowed me to conceive and bring forth a beautiful baby girl Rishae Niger Rucker I called her my miracle baby, because I thought I would never have children again. Eighteen months later I would conceive her sister. Sherrah Kenya Rucker. So now I had two miracle babies, and I was 37 years old. My husband who was on disability at that time related to a previous heart condition had a substance abuse problem. We tried counseling but to no avail. We moved away from my family and support system to be closer to his family in Delaware. A year after the move he passed away related to health conditions and substance abuse. I am conveying to you at the time of his death I did not seek counseling. Not for me or my children which was big mistake. I made emotional and irrational decisions because I did not understand the grief process or the fact that I was dealing with compounded grief. I had lost two husbands in fourteen years of marriage.

Nor did I consider that the children were also grieving. Looking back, I know it was only God's grace and my mother's prayers that kept me sane. I made horrible decisions based on emotion and lack of understanding. This not only affected me but my children. I am amazed that they are the beautiful confident women they are today, as their early years were not one of ease. They each lost father before they reach the age of 8 years old. Because of God's grace they both completed each the bachelor's and master's degrees. My oldest daughter also went one to obtain her bachelor's degree after the death of her father. She also lost her father before the age of eight years. As I said my mother's prayers and my faith in God kept my mind steady. I sometimes wavered because of lack of understanding, yet he is faithful. When my children's father passed away, I continued to pursue my education and service to God. It was a new way of living my single life.

New Beginnings

My mother's health began to fail during my last year in graduate school and I had to relocate again. My children had yet another change in their lives. My middle daughter had just graduated high school. She had a scholarship to the University to Maryland but relinquished it to be with her mother and sister. She did not want to be on the east coast alone while her family was in the Midwest. I thank God that they both achieved their graduate degrees. God is faithful. While working on my graduate degree I met a man that would change the direction and vision of my future. He was from another country and like me had a previous life. But he loved the Lord with all his heart soul and mind. He was little too much like me, as he loved to work both out of necessity and love for his profession. He was one of the most educated and humble men I have ever met. He still had a Liberian accent after 30 years of living in the states. He also loved to garden. He had a beautiful singing voice and a calm speaking voice. He was a gentleman in all aspects of his life. We soon started the have bible studies together and went to fellowship services together. A year after my graduation me asked me to be his wife. This most caring man has blessed the latter half of my life. He believed more than anything else that I would be successful in whatever I put my hand into doing. Our courtship transition from eating out three times a week to me cooking his meals which improved his health. His lab work and demeanor improved with the nurturing he was getting from his new wife. I write this for those who may be contemplating marriage again. "Wait on the Lord and he will give you the desires of your heart. Wait I say on the Lord."

I no longer had to pled for my spouse to attend worship services with me as he was leading me as the King of his home in the ways of the Lord.

Pray on It, Wait on It!

My husband and I were praying for the same thing from two distinct locations. I was praying for a new life some 1500 miles away from him. Two years before I met him. I pray to the Lord for the kind of man I wanted in my life. Many distractions in the form of male pretenders came into my life. I suffered heartbreak related to those who portrayed godliness but denied their power of God. I relocated and started taking care of my mother. My soon to be adult children were in high school and entering college. And I worked sometimes 16- 18 hour shifts to make ends meet. While completing my graduate studies and internship I meet the gentleman from Liberia. He was suffering from an affliction in his body, but he was a sweet man. He walked bent over and appeared to be in pain. However, he did not let that stop him. He asked to meet him in his office at lunch time for bible study. Our friendship grew from there. A few months later we were attending church services and bible studies together. He told me how he was eating the same thing every day to control his Diabetes. I informed him that I could help him with that. We began shopping together and I began preparing his meals. His lab work improved. We started walking together and his posture improved. A few years later we were married. This loving husband of mine lived 1Corthinans 13 for me every day of our life. He has always been kind and gentle with me.

He decided that we should have a home but not go into debt. He had bought a home on auction many years before he met me. It was built in 1920. I must tell when I first saw it, I thought burn it down. My children felt the same way. God intervened and had workers to gut out the house. My husband worked two jobs to pay for supplies to rebuild the house.

He did not want to incur debt. When the house was gutted, he prayed for labors to reconstruct the house. It took a year. Amazingly the workers who prepared the house were paid with my culinary expertise. They would not accept payment for services. The prayers of the righteous availed much as we continue to live in the house this very day. My husband has rebuilt the house, put a tin roof on the house and landscaped the entire property. This is love in action. He and the Lord are the greatest example of the Love of God in my life. My husband encouraged me in my education, counseling, and writing. He supports my ministry and my speaking engagements. He prays for me when I am unable to pray for myself. He builds me up so that I may continue to build him and others up in the work of the Lord. It has never been a competition but a labor of love.

As for me and my house we will serve the Lord!!

Pray Without Ceasing

I have to say one thing here about your prayers. Ask God to give you want you need and not what you want! All that glistens is not gold. I would also advise you to keep a prayer journal so that you can see how God is answering your prayers. It is important for you to maintain a spirit of integrity and brokenness before the Lord. If you want a godly spouse, be specific in your prayers. Do you want someone to lead you in service the lord or just go occasionally to worship on holidays? Do you want him to be filled with the spirit and not the spirit of self-worship? Do you want him to look so good that he spends more time in the mirror than you do? These are concerns that have been brought to me when counseling couples in marriage. Your marriage and your walk with the lord depend upon two things. Hearing from God and having a spirit of repentance. The adversary would love to present you with a counterfeit of what God has in store for you.

Sisters he may be tall dark and handsome, but does he represent God and is a good Stewart of the resources that God has given him? Does he lead with integrity in the church and in his place of business? Does he have a good reputation among his fellow workers or colleagues? I mentioned that when I would go out with my husband he was known for his professionalism and that he was a wonderful professor many say the best they have ever had in college. Twenty years after he stopped teaching, he is recognized in the community as a leader. One thing I noticed about my husband is that is quick to repent. No matter what it is, he will come to me and say I am sorry, I should not have said that. He helped me see that I too needed to repent at times. Let me say this, yes you repent when you come to the lord (salvation), but you also repent when you know that you have wronged or injured your spouse spiritually. It is difficult to walk around with a wounded spirit and serve one another. When I hear couples say that they are not communicating. They just text each other! It saddens me.

My aunt Mildred would say "Lord today!" How is it that we have so many material things but lack the essentials for a happy life in Christ and in marriage. I remember simpler times before cell phones, internet, and the AI. That was the era in which I grew up. You had four television stations if you count PBS. It was not a struggle to get your family to church or even bible study. The church for most was a place of safety and refuge. Most importantly we had the unadulterated pure word of God.

When I prayed for God to send me a husband, I prayed someone to understand who I was as a woman and a child of God. I wanted them to appreciate my heritage in Christ and my lineage. I prayed that I would have someone who would support me in my spiritual and professional development. I wanted that iron sharped iron person in my life.

My husband has stepped into many roles in my life. He is my best friend, a mentor, a spiritual advisor, leader in the kingdom of God and a wonderful father for my children. He at times has been my business partner and advisor. He is an organizer and a planner. God knew I needed that. He is a visionary. When people were telling him to burn down the house, he bought at auction he saw the potential in what God had in store for us.

I prayed that God would give me what I needed not what I wanted. God is faithful!!

Epilogue

If I had read this book at age 18 or 19, it might have changed the vision that had for myself up to as a naïve young woman. Growing up only knowing church and not life, ill prepared me for the world I was venturing off into at age 18. As I said, I knew church rules regulations and traditions. but did not know life or the pitfalls that awaited a young naïve woman. I lost my father when I was 18 years old. He would have been my protector. My mother was overwhelmed with her own loss and raising three younger children. I had no father figure or uncle that lived close enough to step in as a protector. I thank God every day that my mother prayed for me knowing how ill prepared I was for the world living in the concrete jungle. Satan was prowling around every street and highway to devour me. I praised God that in all of this he kept me from drugs and a life on the streets. I had no education to speaking of at age 18, other than a high school diploma, and the plans of the enemy were clear. He wanted to use me for his kingdom. When I felt the fiery darts of the enemy I (ran to the church. It did not matter what church. I discerned that I needed to be covered by the blood of Jesus. I had visons that would make the hairs on my arms stand up. I knew the enemy was after my soul, but I also Knew God had a plan for my life and that no weapon formed against me would prosper.

God won the war and the battle. Praise the Lord!

About the Author

Mrs. Shelia T. Cisco is the eldest daughter of Dr. Johnnie B, Wilson (deceased)and Ethel Mae Wilson- Miller. She is married to Rev. Washington Cisco. The share six children in a blended family. They work in ministry together, as counselors and ministers. Mrs. Cisco loves to sing and works in her area in nursing home ministry and visitation. She and her co- laborer in the counseling Cathy Baker have founded a caregiver support group "Compassion of Caregivers "in 2024.

Mrs. Cisco has authored three other books. "Of Vision and Dreams for Her Daughters "in 2021, published by Dorrance Publishing. She also authored a children's book entitled "Sir Gregory the Groundhog of Essex County" in 2023 by Christian faith Publishing, and "Loving the Broken in 2024" self-published.

She is a licensed professional counselor in the state of Illinois and a Divorce Mediator approved by the Illinois and Missouri Supreme Court. She was previously a nurse and educator for 30 years. She is an ordained minister of the Gospel. Her ministry to the lost and forgotten is her passion. She enjoys gardening, cooking, and traveling. She is currently a member of the American Counseling association and a Member of the American Adults with Disabilities Association. She and her co- founder Cathy Baker started a group to address the needs of care givers coping with spouses who have disabilities, it is called Compassion for Caregivers.

She resides in Southern Illinois with her loving husband Rev. Washington D. Cisco.

Printed in the United States
by Baker & Taylor Publisher Services